You are Enough

BY BROOKE BUTLER

You Are Enough
Brooke Butler

Illustrated by Fx and Color Studio

Published by
True Vine Publishing Company
810 Dominican
Dr. Nashville, TN 37228
www.TrueVinePublishing.org

ISBN: 978-1-968092-55-9 Paperback

ISBN: 978-1-968092-56-6

Printed in the United States of America-First Print

Dedication:

This book is dedicated to my mom Dr. Monique Butler and my grandmothers, Theresa Mae Grant and Vivian Lee Butler. Thank you for instilling in me what it takes to be a phenomenal woman.

I stood in front of the mirror one morning.
Someone stood there too.
She looked just like me.
Same eyes, some hair,
but her face felt tight and serious.

Her voice was soft at first,
like she was helping.
Then it got louder; bossier.

I tried to tell her,
"I'm doing my best."
but she didn't listen.
She only wanted to talk.

So I listened.
For some reason,
I felt bad for her.

Every day, she pointed things out.
Too messy,
too slow
too different.

She pulled at my thoughts before they could grow. She said she was making me better.

One day, I looked closely into her eyes.
Something felt...strange.
I had seen that look before.
Worried.
Tired.
Afraid of getting things wrong.

I took a deep breath.
And suddenly, everything went quiet.

The mirror didn't shout.
It didn't whisper.
It waited.

In the quiet, I understood.
She wasn't trying to hurt me.
She was my worry.
Wearing my face.
Using my voice.

I gently touched the mirror.
She didn't move because
she wasn't really there.
She was inside me.

I closed my eyes.
I listened past the worry.
Behind all the noise,
there was something else.

Not anger.
Not judgement.
Kindness.

I opened my eyes and smiled.
"Thank you for trying to protect me,"
I said. "But I'm okay."

The mirror felt lighter.

I stood a little taller.
not because I was perfect,
but because I finally heard the truth.

You Are Enough